Piano • Vocal • Guitar

SMOKEY ROBINSON
SHEET MUSIC COLLECTION

ISBN 978-1-5400-1233-3

HAL•LEONARD®
7777 W. BLUEMOUND RD. P.O. BOX 13819 MILWAUKEE, WI 53213

In Australia Contact:
Hal Leonard Australia Pty. Ltd.
4 Lentara Court
Cheltenham, Victoria, 3192 Australia
Email: ausadmin@halleonard.com.au

Visit Hal Leonard Online at
www.halleonard.com

CONTENTS

AIN'T THAT PECULIAR

Words and Music by ROBERT ROGERS,
WILLIAM ROBINSON, JR., MARVIN TARPLIN
and WARREN MOORE

* Recorded a half step lower.

BEING WITH YOU

Words and Music by
WILLIAM "SMOKEY" ROBINSON

I don't care what they think _____ a - bout me, and _____
I don't care if they start _____ to a - void me; _____

I don't care what they say. _____
I don't care what they do. _____

I don't care what they think _____
I don't care a - bout an -

Optional repeat of 8 bar Intro. (Instr. solo) before 2nd Verse.

CRUISIN'

Words and Music by WILLIAM "SMOKEY" ROBINSON
and MARVIN TARPLIN

Moderately slow

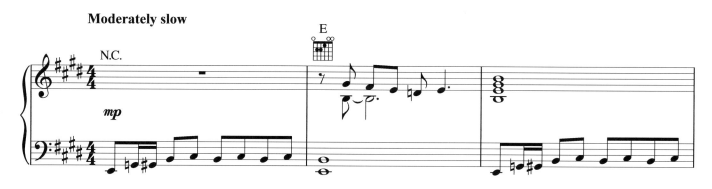

Ba - by, let's cruise a - way from
Ba - by, to - night be - longs to
Ba - by, let's cruise, let's float, let's

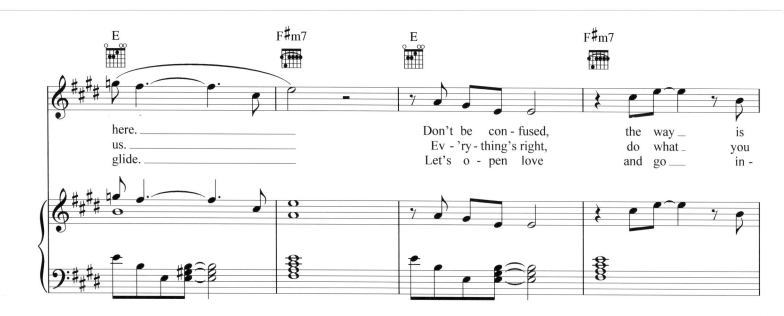

here. Don't be con - fused, the way is
us. Ev - 'ry - thing's right, do what you
glide. Let's o - pen love and go in -

GET READY

Words and Music by
WILLIAM "SMOKEY" ROBINSON

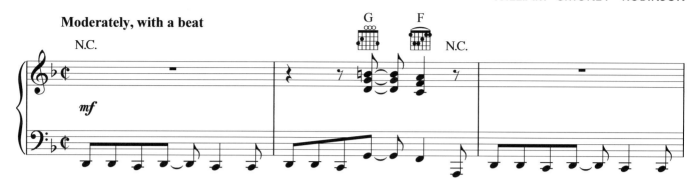

JUST TO SEE HER

Words and Music by JIMMY GEORGE
and LOU PARDINI

GOING TO A GO-GO

Words and Music by WILLIAM "SMOKEY" ROBINSON,
MARVIN TARPLIN, WARREN MOORE and ROBERT ROGERS

I SECOND THAT EMOTION

Words and Music by WILLIAM "SMOKEY" ROBINSON
and ALFRED CLEVELAND

MORE LOVE

Words and Music by
WILLIAM "SMOKEY" ROBINSON

ONE HEARTBEAT

Words and Music by STEVE LEGASSICK
and BRIAN RAY

some-thing so eas - y make me feel so com-plete? ___ Take it

D.S. al Coda

CODA

One ___ heart - beat. Take it eas-y.

Ooh, I want to feel your ev-'ry e - mo - tion.

Shh, don't talk, and we'll be mak-ing love in

MY GIRL

Words and Music by SMOKEY ROBINSON
and RONALD WHITE

(Talk - in' 'bout my girl, my girl,

e - ven got the month of May with my girl. _____

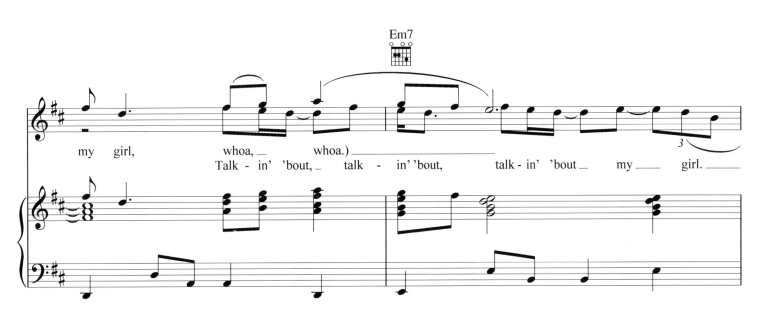

my girl, whoa, _ whoa.) _____

Talk - in' 'bout, _ talk - in' 'bout, talk - in' 'bout _ my _ girl. _____

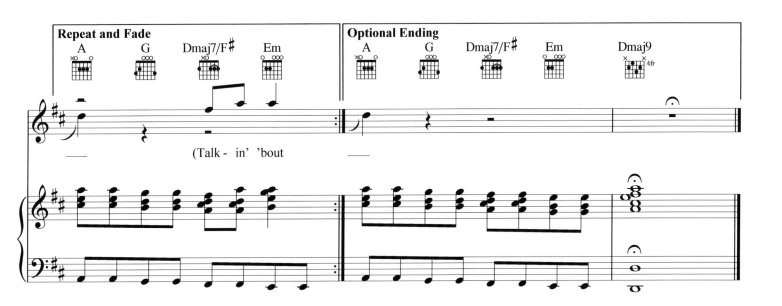

(Talk - in' 'bout _____

OOO BABY BABY

Words and Music by WILLIAM "SMOKEY" ROBINSON
and WARREN MOORE

Slowly

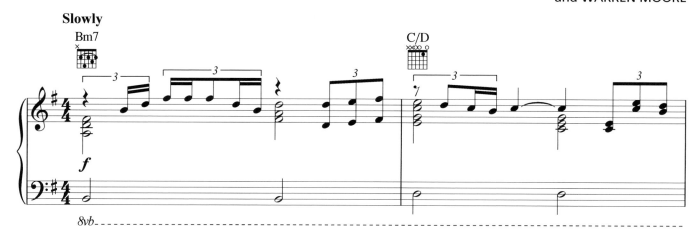

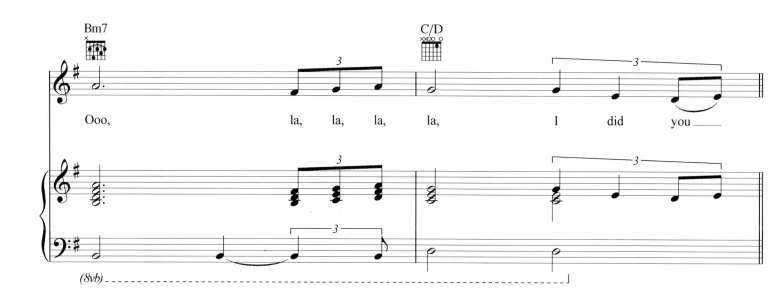

Ooo, la, la, la, la, I did you

wrong; ___ my heart ___ went out to play, and in the game, ___ I
takes, ___ I know ___ I've made a few, but I'm on - ly

Ooo,

ba - by, ba - by.
ba - by, ba - by. ___ Ooo, ___

To Coda ⊕

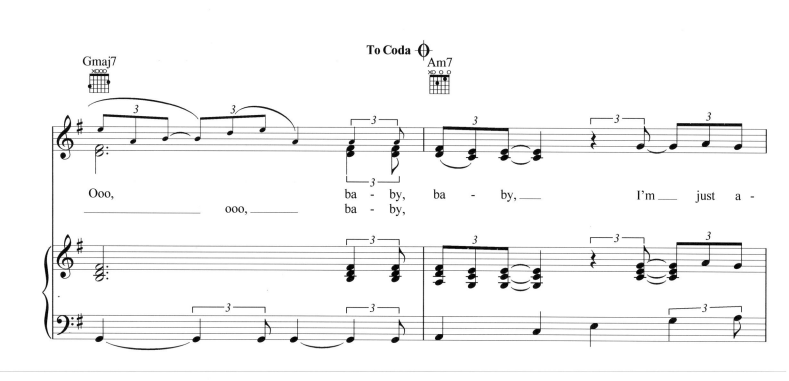

Ooo,

___ ooo, ___
ba - by, ba - by, ___ I'm ___ just a-
ba - by,

bout ___ at ___ the end of my rope. ___ But I can't stop

QUIET STORM

Words and Music by
WILLIAM "SMOKEY" ROBINSON
and ROSE ELLA JONES

Moderately, with a beat

Soft and

warm,   a qui-et storm,   qui-et
sigh   weak am I,   a but-ter-fly

as when flow-ers talk at break of dawn.   break of
caught up in a hur-ri-cane.   hur-ri-

THE TEARS OF A CLOWN

Words and Music by STEVIE WONDER,
WILLIAM "SMOKEY" ROBINSON and HENRY COSBY

Additional Lyrics

Now, if there's a smile on my face
Don't let my glad expression
Give you a wrong impression
Don't let this smile I wear
Make you think that I don't care. *(Fade)*

SHOP AROUND

Words and Music by BERRY GORDY JR.
and SMOKEY ROBINSON

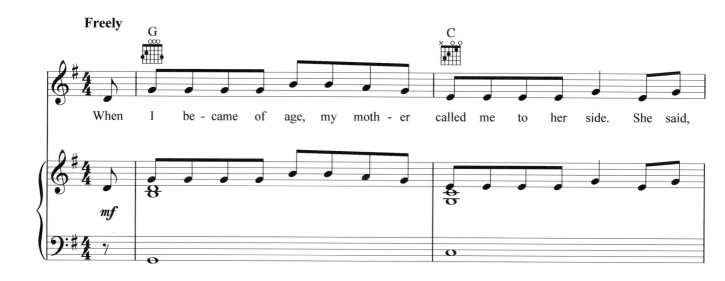

When I be-came of age, my moth-er called me to her side. She said,

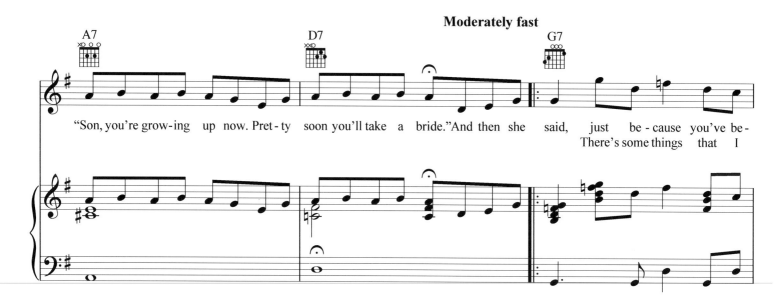

"Son, you're grow-ing up now. Pret-ty soon you'll take a bride." And then she said, just be-cause you've be-
There's some things that I

come a young man now, there's still some things that you don't un-der-stand now.
want you to know now. Just as sure as the wind's gon-na blow now,

THE TRACKS OF MY TEARS

Words and Music by SMOKEY ROBINSON,
WARREN MOORE and MARVIN TARPLIN

put me down.____ My smile is my make-up I wear since my break-up with

you. Ba-by, take a good____ look at my face. You'll see my

smile____ looks out of place. Yeah, just look clos-er,____ it's eas-y to

Repeat and Fade

trace the tracks of my tears,____ ba-by, ba-by, ba-by, ba-by. Take a

THE WAY YOU DO THE THINGS YOU DO

Words and Music by WILLIAM "SMOKEY" ROBINSON
and ROBERT ROGERS

YOU'VE REALLY GOT A HOLD ON ME

Words and Music by
WILLIAM "SMOKEY" ROBINSON

I don't _____ like you, _____ but I _____ love you;
I don't _____ want you, _____ but I _____ need you;
I wan - na leave you, _____ don't wan - na stay here;

seems that I'm al - ways _____ think - ing of you. _____
don't wan - na kiss you, _____ but I _____ need to. _____
don't wan - na spend _____ an - oth - er day here. _____

hold ____ on __ me. __ Ba - by, ____
(You real - ly got a hold on me.)

I love __ you and all I want __ you to do is just hold _ me, hold _ me,
hold _ me, (please) _ hold _ me, (squeeze) _

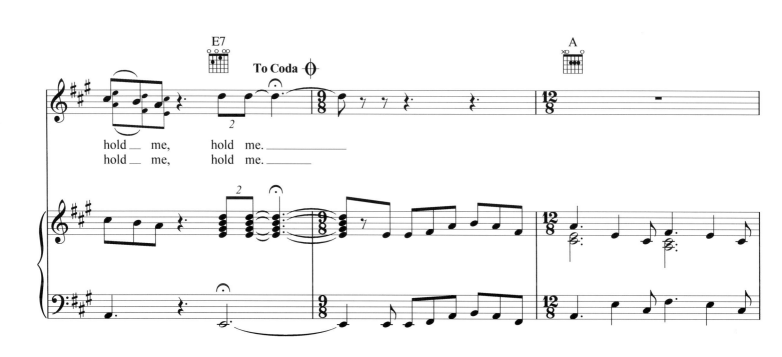

hold _ me, hold me. ____
hold _ me, hold me. ____